Positioning in CSS
Layout Enhancements for the Web

Eric A. Meyer

Beijing · Boston · Farnham · Sebastopol · Tokyo

Positioning in CSS

by Eric A. Meyer

Printed in the United States of America.

Published by O'Reilly Media, Inc., 1005 Gravenstein Highway North, Sebastopol, CA 95472.

O'Reilly books may be purchased for educational, business, or sales promotional use. Online editions are also available for most titles (*http://safaribooksonline.com*). For more information, contact our corporate/institutional sales department: 800-998-9938 or *corporate@oreilly.com*.

Editor: Meg Foley	**Interior Designer:** David Futato
Production Editor: Colleen Lobner	**Cover Designer:** Ellie Volckhausen
Copyeditor: Amanda Kersey	**Illustrator:** Rebecca Demarest
Proofreader: Molly Ives Brower	

April 2016:   First Edition

Revision History for the First Edition

2016-04-11:   First Release

See *http://oreilly.com/catalog/errata.csp?isbn=9781491930373* for release details.

978-1-491-93037-3

[LSI]

Table of Contents

Preface

Conventions Used in This Book

The following typographical conventions are used in this book:

Italic
> Indicates new terms, URLs, email addresses, filenames, and file extensions.

`Constant width`
> Used for program listings, as well as within paragraphs to refer to program elements such as variable or function names, databases, data types, environment variables, statements, and keywords.

`Constant width bold`
> Shows commands or other text that should be typed literally by the user.

`Constant width italic`
> Shows text that should be replaced with user-supplied values or by values determined by context.

 This element signifies a general note.

 This element indicates a warning or caution.

Safari® Books Online

 *Safari Books Online* is an on-demand digital library that delivers expert content in both book and video form from the world's leading authors in technology and business.

Technology professionals, software developers, web designers, and business and creative professionals use Safari Books Online as their primary resource for research, problem solving, learning, and certification training.

Safari Books Online offers a range of plans and pricing for enterprise, government, education, and individuals.

Members have access to thousands of books, training videos, and prepublication manuscripts in one fully searchable database from publishers like O'Reilly Media, Prentice Hall Professional, Addison-Wesley Professional, Microsoft Press, Sams, Que, Peachpit Press, Focal Press, Cisco Press, John Wiley & Sons, Syngress, Morgan Kaufmann, IBM Redbooks, Packt, Adobe Press, FT Press, Apress, Manning, New Riders, McGraw-Hill, Jones & Bartlett, Course Technology, and hundreds more. For more information about Safari Books Online, please visit us online.

How to Contact Us

Please address comments and questions concerning this book to the publisher:

> O'Reilly Media, Inc.
> 1005 Gravenstein Highway North
> Sebastopol, CA 95472
> 800-998-9938 (in the United States or Canada)
> 707-829-0515 (international or local)
> 707-829-0104 (fax)

We have a web page for this book, where we list errata, examples, and any additional information. You can access this page at *http://bit.ly/positioning-in-css*.

To comment or ask technical questions about this book, send email to *bookquestions@oreilly.com*.

For more information about our books, courses, conferences, and news, see our website at *http://www.oreilly.com*.

Find us on Facebook: *http://facebook.com/oreilly*

Follow us on Twitter: *http://twitter.com/oreillymedia*

Watch us on YouTube: *http://www.youtube.com/oreillymedia*

Positioning

The idea behind positioning is fairly simple. It allows you to define exactly where element boxes will appear relative to where they would ordinarily be—or position them in relation to a parent element, another element, or even to the viewport (e.g., the browser window) itself.

Basic Concepts

Before we delve into the various kinds of positioning, it's a good idea to look at what types exist and how they differ. We'll also need to define some basic ideas that are fundamental to understanding how positioning works.

Types of Positioning

You can choose one of five different types of positioning, which affect how the element's box is generated, by using the `position` property.

position

Values:	`static｜relative｜sticky｜absolute｜fixed｜inherit`
Initial value:	`static`
Applies to:	All elements
Inherited:	No
Computed value:	As specified

The values of `position` have the following meanings:

`static`
> The element's box is generated as normal. Block-level elements generate a rectangular box that is part of the document's flow, and inline-level boxes cause the creation of one or more line boxes that are flowed within their parent element.

`relative`
> The element's box is offset by some distance. The element retains the shape it would have had were it not positioned, and the space that the element would ordinarily have occupied is preserved.

`absolute`
> The element's box is completely removed from the flow of the document and positioned with respect to its containing block, which may be another element in the document or the initial containing block (described in the next section). Whatever space the element might have occupied in the normal document flow is closed up, as though the element did not exist. The positioned element generates a block-level box, regardless of the type of box it would have generated if it were in the normal flow.

`fixed`
> The element's box behaves as though it was set to `absolute`, but its containing block is the viewport itself.

`sticky`
> The element is left in the normal flow until the conditions that trigger its stickiness come to pass, at which point it is removed from the normal flow but its original space in the normal flow is preserved. It will then act as if absolutely positioned with respect to its containing block. Once the conditions to enforce stickiness are no longer met, the element is returned to the normal flow in its original space.

Don't worry so much about the details right now, as we'll look at each of these kinds of positioning later. Before we do that, we need to discuss containing blocks.

The Containing Block

In general terms, a *containing block* is the box that contains another element. As an example, in the normal-flow case, the root element (`html` in HTML) is the containing block for the body element, which is in turn the containing block for all its children, and so on. When it comes to positioning, the containing block depends entirely on the type of positioning.

For a non-root element whose position value is relative or static, its containing block is formed by the content edge of the nearest block-level, table-cell, or inline-block ancestor box.

For a non-root element that has a position value of absolute, its containing block is set to the nearest ancestor (of any kind) that has a position value other than static. This happens as follows:

- If the ancestor is block-level, the containing block is set to be that element's padding edge; in other words, the area that would be bounded by a border.
- If the ancestor is inline-level, the containing block is set to the content edge of the ancestor. In left-to-right languages, the top and left of the containing block are the top and left content edges of the first box in the ancestor, and the bottom and right edges are the bottom and right content edges of the last box. In right-to-left languages, the right edge of the containing block corresponds to the right content edge of the first box, and the left is taken from the last box. The top and bottom are the same.
- If there are no ancestors, then the element's containing block is defined to be the initial containing block.

There's an interesting variant to the containing-block rules when it comes to sticky-positioned elements, which is that a rectangle is defined in relation to the containing block called the *sticky-constraint rectangle*. This rectangle has everything to do with how sticky positioning works, and will be explained in full later, in "Sticky Positioning" on page 36.

An important point: positioned elements can be positioned outside of their containing block. This is very similar to the way in which floated elements can use negative margins to float outside of their parent's content area. It also suggests that the term "containing block" should really be "positioning context," but since the specification uses "containing block," so will I. (I do try to minimize confusion. Really!)

Offset Properties

Four of the positioning schemes described in the previous section—relative, absolute, sticky, and fixed—use four distinct properties to describe the offset of a positioned element's sides with respect to its containing block. These four properties, which are referred to as the *offset properties*, are a big part of what makes positioning work.

top, right, bottom, left

Values:	\<length> | \<percentage> | auto | inherit
Initial value:	auto
Applies to:	Positioned elements
Inherited:	No
Percentages:	Refer to the height of the containing block for top and bottom, and the width of the containing block for right and left
Computed value:	For relative or sticky-positioned elements, see the sections on those positioning types. For static elements, auto; for length values, the corresponding absolute length; for percentage values, the specified value; otherwise, auto

These properties describe an offset from the nearest side of the containing block (thus the term *offset properties*). For example, top describes how far the top margin edge of the positioned element should be placed from the top of its containing block. In the case of top, positive values move the top margin edge of the positioned element *downward*, while negative values move it *above* the top of its containing block. Similarly, left describes how far to the right (for positive values) or left (for negative values) the left margin edge of the positioned element is from the left edge of the containing block. Positive values will shift the margin edge of the positioned element to the right, and negative values will move it to the left.

Another way to look at it is that positive values cause inward offsets, moving the edges toward the center of the containing block, and negative values cause outward offsets.

The implication of offsetting the margin edges of a positioned element is that everything about an element—margins, borders, padding, and content—is moved in the process[of positioning the element. Thus, it is possible to set margins, borders, and padding for a positioned element; these will be preserved and kept with the positioned element, and they will be contained within the area defined by the offset properties.

It is important to remember that the offset properties define an offset from the analogous side (e.g., left defines the offset from the left side) of the containing block, not from the upper-left corner of the containing block. This is why, for example, one way to fill up the lower-right corner of a containing block is to use these values:

```
top: 50%; bottom: 0; left: 50%; right: 0;
```

In this example, the outer-left edge of the positioned element is placed halfway across the containing block. This is its offset from the left edge of the containing block. The outer-right edge of the positioned element, however, is not offset from the right edge of the containing block, so the two are coincident. Similar reasoning holds true for the top and bottom of the positioned element: the outer-top edge is placed halfway down the containing block, but the outer-bottom edge is not moved up from the bottom. This leads to what's shown in Figure 1.

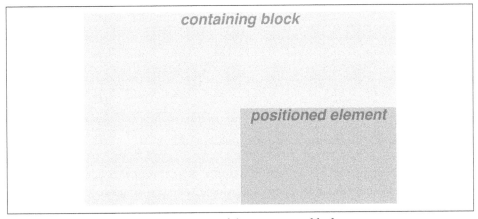

Figure 1. Filling the lower-right quarter of the containing block

 What's depicted in Figure 1, and in most of the examples in this chapter, is based around absolute positioning. Since absolute positioning is the simplest scheme in which to demonstrate how top, right, bottom, and left work, we'll stick to that for now.

Note the background area of the positioned element. In Figure 1, it has no margins, but if it did, they would create blank space between the borders and the offset edges. This would make the positioned element appear as though it did not completely fill the lower-right quarter of the containing block. In truth, it *would* fill the area, but this fact wouldn't be immediately apparent to the eye. Thus, the following two sets of styles would have approximately the same visual appearance, assuming that the containing block is 100em high by 100em wide:

```
top: 50%; bottom: 0; left: 50%; right: 0; margin: 10em;
top: 60%; bottom: 10%; left: 60%; right: 10%; margin: 0;
```

Again, the similarity would be only visual in nature.

By using negative offset values, it is possible to position an element outside its containing block. For example, the following values will lead to the result shown in Figure 2:

```
top: 50%; bottom: -2em; left: 75%; right: -7em;
```

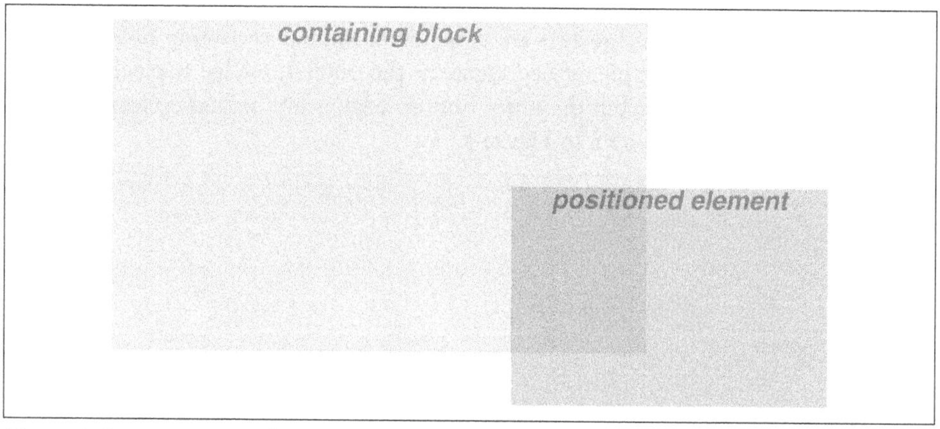

Figure 2. Positioning an element outside its containing block

In addition to length and percentage values, the offset properties can also be set to auto, which is the default value. There is no single behavior for auto; it changes based on the type of positioning used. We'll explore how auto works later on, as we consider each of the positioning types in turn.

Width and Height

There will be many cases when, having determined where you're going to position an element, you will want to declare how wide and how high that element should be. In addition, there will likely be conditions where you'll want to limit how high or wide a positioned element gets, not to mention cases where you want the browser to go ahead and automatically calculate the width, height, or both.

Setting Width and Height

If you want to give your positioned element a specific width, then the obvious property to turn to is width. Similarly, height will let you declare a specific height for a positioned element.

Although it is sometimes important to set the width and height of an element, it is not always necessary when positioning elements. For example, if the placement of the four sides of the element is described using top, right, bottom, and left, then the height and width of the element are implicitly determined by the offsets. Assume that we want an absolutely positioned element to fill the left half of its containing block, from top to bottom. We could use these values, with the result depicted in Figure 3:

```
top: 0; bottom: 0; left: 0; right: 50%;
```

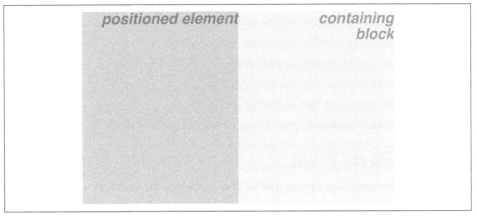

Figure 3. Positioning and sizing an element using only the offset properties

Since the default value of both width and height is auto, the result shown in Figure 3 is exactly the same as if we had used these values:

```
top: 0; bottom: 0; left: 0; right: 50%; width: 50%; height: 100%;
```

The presence of width and height in this example add nothing to the layout of the element.

Of course, if we were to add padding, a border, or a margin to the element, then the presence of explicit values for height and width could very well make a difference:

```
top: 0; bottom: 0; left: 0; right: 50%; width: 50%; height: 100%;
    padding: 2em;
```

This will give us a positioned element that extends out of its containing block, as shown in Figure 4.

This happens because (by default) the padding is added to the content area, and the content area's size is determined by the values of height and width. In order to get the padding we want and still have the element fit inside its containing block, we would either remove the height and width declarations, explicitly set them both to auto, or set box-sizing to border-box.

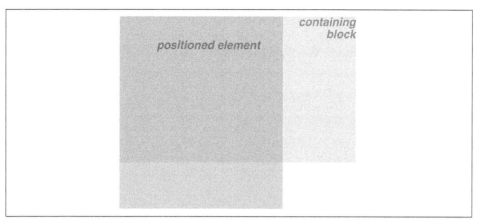

Figure 4. Positioning an element partially outside its containing block

Limiting Width and Height

Should it become necessary or desirable, you can place limits on an element's width by using the following properties, which I'll refer to as the *min-max properties*. An element's content area can be defined to have minimum dimensions using `min-width` and `min-height`.

min-width, min-height	
Values:	<length> | <percentage> | `inherit`
Initial value:	`0`
Applies to:	All elements except nonreplaced inline elements and table elements
Inherited:	No
Percentages:	Refer to the width of the containing block
Computed value:	For percentages, as specified; for length values, the absolute length; otherwise, none

Similarly, an element's dimensions can be limited using the properties `max-width` and `max-height`.

max-width, max-height

Values:	<length> | <percentage> | none | `inherit`
Initial value:	none
Applies to:	All elements except nonreplaced inline elements and table elements
Inherited:	No
Percentages:	Refer to the height of the containing block
Computed value:	For percentages, as specified; for length values, the absolute length; otherwise, none

The names of these properties make them fairly self-explanatory. What's less obvious at first, but makes sense once you think about it, is that values for all these properties cannot be negative.

The following styles will force the positioned element to be at least 10em wide by 20em tall, as illustrated in Figure 5:

```
top: 10%; bottom: 20%; left: 50%; right: 10%;
    min-width: 10em; min-height: 20em;
```

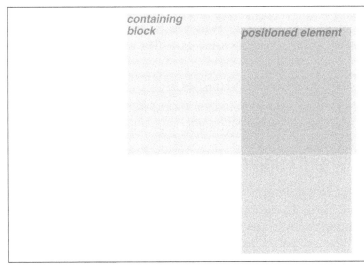

Figure 5. Setting a minimum width and height for a positioned element

This isn't a very robust solution since it forces the element to be at least a certain size regardless of the size of its containing block. Here's a better one:

```
top: 10%; bottom: auto; left: 50%; right: 10%;
    height: auto; min-width: 15em;
```

Here we have a case where the element should be 40% as wide as the containing block but can never be less than 15em wide. We've also changed the bottom and height so that they're automatically determined. This will let the element be as tall as necessary to display its content, no matter how narrow it gets (never less than 15em, of course!).

 We'll look at the role auto plays in the height and width of positioned elements in an upcoming section.

You can turn all this around to keep elements from getting too wide or tall by using max-width and max-height. Let's consider a situation where, for some reason, we want an element to have three-quarters the width of its containing block but to stop getting wider when it hits 400 pixels. The appropriate styles are:

```
left: 0%; right: auto; width: 75%; max-width: 400px;
```

One great advantage of the min-max properties is that they let you mix units with relative safety. You can use percentage-based sizes while setting length-based limits, or vice versa.

It's worth mentioning that these min-max properties can be very useful in conjunction with floated elements. For example, we can allow a floated element's width to be relative to the width of its parent element (which is its containing block), while making sure that the float's width never goes below 10em. The reverse approach is also possible:

```
p.aside {float: left; width: 40em; max-width: 40%;}
```

This will set the float to be 40em wide, unless that would be more than 40% the width of the containing block, in which case the float will be limited to that 40% width.

Content Overflow and Clipping

If the content of an element is too much for the element's size, it will be in danger of overflowing the element itself. There are a few alternatives in such situations, and CSS lets you select among them. It also allows you to define a clipping region to determine the area of the element outside of which these sorts of things become an issue.

Overflow

So let's say that we have, for whatever reason, an element that has been pinned to a specific size, and the content doesn't fit. You can take control of the situation with the overflow property.

overflow	
Values:	visible|hidden|scroll|auto|inherit
Initial value:	visible
Applies to:	Block-level and replaced elements
Inherited:	No
Computed value:	As specified

The default value of visible means that the element's content may be visible outside the element's box. Typically, this leads to the content simply running outside its own element box but not altering the shape of that box. The following markup would result in Figure 6:

```
div#sidebar {position: absolute; top: 0; left: 0; width: 25%; height: 7em;
    background: #BBB; overflow: visible;}
```

If overflow is set to scroll, the element's content is clipped—that is, hidden—at the edges of the element box, but there is some way to make the extra content available to the user. In a web browser, this could mean a scroll bar (or set of them), or another method of accessing the content without altering the shape of the element itself. One possibility is depicted in Figure 7, which results from the following markup:

```
div#sidebar {position: absolute; top: 0; left: 0; width: 15%; height: 7em;
    overflow: scroll;}
```

If scroll is used, the panning mechanisms (e.g., scroll bars) should always be rendered. To quote the specification, "this avoids any problem with scrollbars appearing or disappearing in a dynamic environment." Thus, even if the element has sufficient space to display all its content, the scroll bars should still appear. In addition, when printing a page or otherwise displaying the document in a print medium, the content may be displayed as though the value of overflow were declared to be visible.

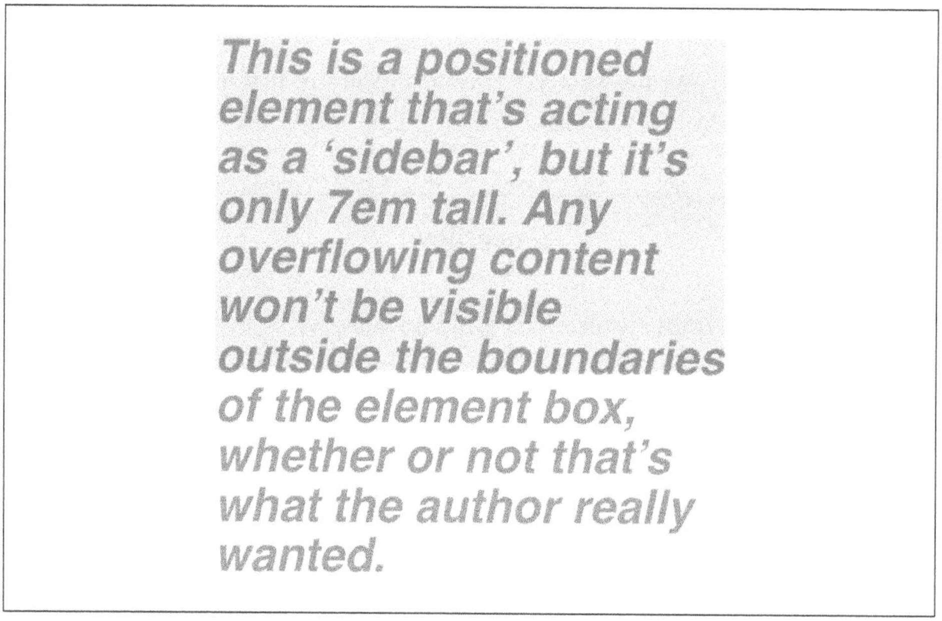

Figure 6. Content visibly overflowing the element box

If `overflow` is set to `hidden`, the element's content is clipped at the edges of the element box, but no scrolling interface should be provided to make the content outside the clipping region accessible to the user. Consider the following markup:

```
div#sidebar {position: absolute; top: 0; left: 0; width: 15%; height: 7em;
    overflow: hidden;}
```

In such an instance, the clipped content would not be accessible to the user. This would lead to a situation like that illustrated in Figure 8.

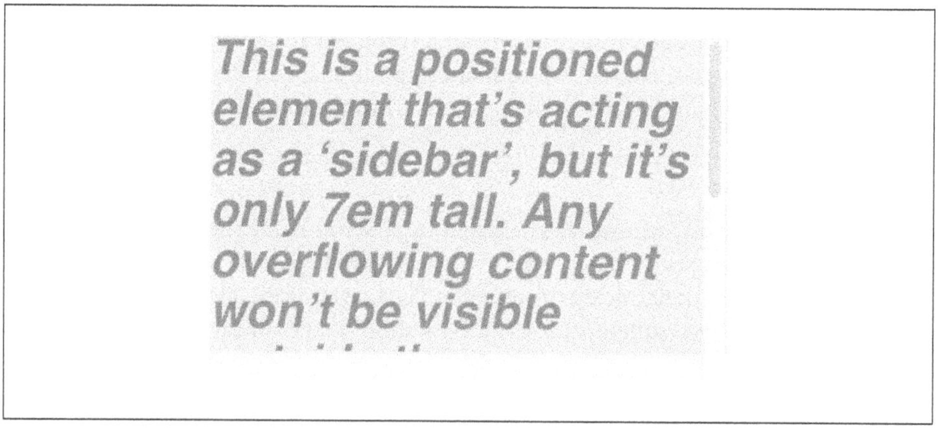

Figure 7. Overflowing content made available via a scroll mechanism

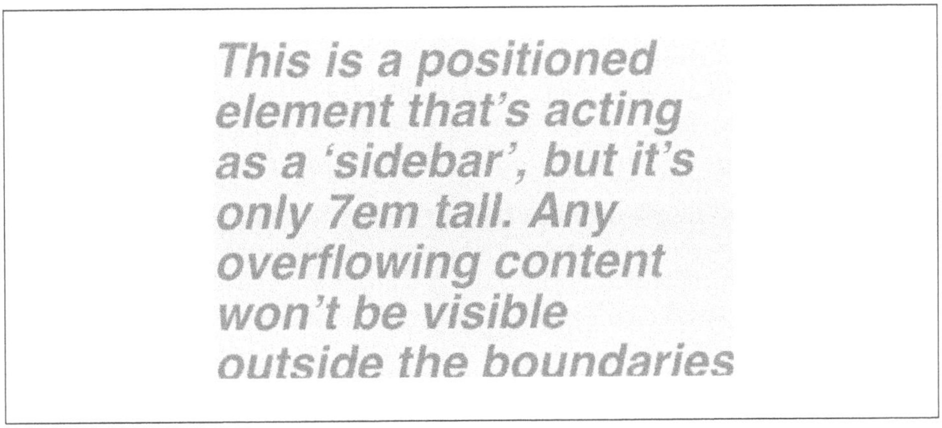

Figure 8. Clipping content at the edges of the content area

Finally, there is overflow: auto. This allows user agents to determine which behavior to use, although they are encouraged to provide a scrolling mechanism when necessary. This is a potentially useful way to use overflow, since user agents could interpret it to mean "provide scroll bars only when needed." (They may not, but they certainly could and probably should.)

Element Visibility

In addition to all the clipping and overflowing, you can also control the visibility of an entire element.

visibility	
Values:	visible | hidden | collapse | inherit
Initial value:	visible
Applies to:	All elements
Inherited:	Yes
Computed value:	As specified

This one is pretty easy. If an element is set to have `visibility: visible`, then it is, of course, visible. If an element is set to `visibility: hidden`, it is made "invisible" (to use the wording in the specification). In its invisible state, the element still affects the document's layout as though it were `visible`. In other words, the element is still there —you just can't see it, pretty much as if you'd declared `opacity: 0`.

Note the difference between this and `display: none`. In the latter case, the element is not displayed *and* is removed from the document altogether so that it doesn't have any effect on document layout. Figure 9 shows a document in which a paragraph has been set to `hidden`, based on the following styles and markup:

```
em.trans {visibility: hidden; border: 3px solid gray; background: silver;
    margin: 2em; padding: 1em;}

<p>
    This is a paragraph which should be visible. Nulla berea consuetudium ohio
    city, mutationem dolore. <em class="trans">Humanitatis molly shannon
    ut lorem.</em> Doug dieken dolor possim south euclid.
</p>
```

This is a paragraph which should be visible. Nulla berea consuetudium ohio city, mutationem dolore.

Doug

dieken dolor possim south euclid.

Figure 9. Making elements invisible without suppressing their element boxes

Everything visible about a hidden element—such as content, background, and borders—is made invisible. The space is still there because the element is still part of the document's layout. We just can't see it.

It's possible to set the descendant element of a `hidden` element to be `visible`. This causes the element to appear wherever it normally would, despite the fact that the ancestor is invisible. In order to do so, we explicitly declare the descendant element `visible`, since `visibility` is inherited:

```
p.clear {visibility: hidden;}
p.clear em {visibility: visible;}
```

As for `visbility: collapse`, this value is used in CSS table rendering, which we don't really have room to cover here. According to the specification, `collapse` has the same meaning as `hidden` if it is used on nontable elements.

Absolute Positioning

Since most of the examples and figures in the previous sections are examples of absolute positioning, you're already halfway to understanding how it works. Most of what remains are the details of what happens when absolute positioning is invoked.

Containing Blocks and Absolutely Positioned Elements

When an element is positioned absolutely, it is completely removed from the document flow. It is then positioned with respect to its containing block, and its margin edges are placed using the offset properties (`top`, `left`, etc.). The positioned element does not flow around the content of other elements, nor does their content flow around the positioned element. This implies that an absolutely positioned element may overlap other elements or be overlapped by them. (We'll see how to affect the overlapping order later.)

The containing block for an absolutely positioned element is the nearest ancestor element that has a `position` value other than `static`. It is common for an author to pick an element that will serve as the containing block for the absolutely positioned element and give it a `position` of `relative` with no offsets, like so:

```
.contain {position: relative;}
```

Consider the example in Figure 10, which is an illustration of the following:

```
p {margin: 2em;}
p.contain {position: relative;} /* establish a containing block*/
b {position: absolute; top: auto; right: 0; bottom: 0; left: auto;
    width: 8em; height: 5em; border: 1px solid gray;}

<body>
<p>
    This paragraph does <em>not</em> establish a containing block for any of
    its descendant elements that are absolutely positioned. Therefore, the
    absolutely positioned <b>boldface</b> element it contains will be
    positioned with respect to the initial containing block.
</p>
<p class="contain">
    Thanks to <code>position: relative</code>, this paragraph establishes a
    containing block for any of its descendant elements that are absolutely
    positioned. Since there is such an element-- <em>that is to say, <b>a
    boldfaced element that is absolutely positioned,</b> placed with respect
    to its containing block (the paragraph)</em>, it will appear within the
    element box generated by the paragraph.
</p>
</body>
```

The b elements in both paragraphs have been absolutely positioned. The difference is in the containing block used for each one. The b element in the first paragraph is positioned with respect to the initial containing block, because all of its ancestor elements have a `position` of `static`. The second paragraph has been set to `position: relative`, so it establishes a containing block for its descendants.

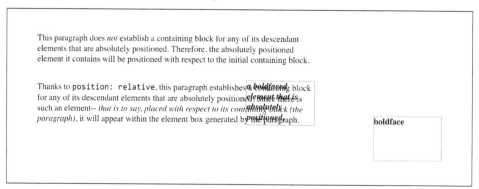

Figure 10. Using relative positioning to define containing blocks

You've probably noted that in that second paragraph, the positioned element overlaps some of the text content of the paragraph. There is no way to avoid this, short of positioning the b element outside of the paragraph (by using a negative value for `right` or one of the other offset properties) or by specifying a padding for the paragraph that is wide enough to accommodate the positioned element. Also, since the b element has a transparent background, the paragraph's text shows through the positioned element. The only way to avoid this is to set a background for the positioned element, or else move it out of the paragraph entirely.

You will sometimes want to ensure that the body element establishes a containing block for all its descendants, rather than allowing the user agent to pick an initial containing block. This is as simple as declaring:

```
body {position: relative;}
```

In such a document, you could drop in an absolutely positioned paragraph, as follows, and get a result like that shown in Figure 11:

```
<p style="position: absolute; top: 0; right: 25%; left: 25%; bottom:
    auto; width: 50%; height: auto; background: silver;">
    ...
</p>
```

The paragraph is now positioned at the very beginning of the document, half as wide as the document's width and overwriting other content.

Once the competit   It could be worse. Just imagine if she   1 alone, and they never
notice the facial color o were a proctologist.   're trapped at a
midwifery party when the games begin. They just keep topping each other with tales of
pregnancies with more complications and bigger emergencies, as though it were the most
natural thing in the world, until the stories involve more gore and slime than any three David
Cronenberg movies put together, with a little bit of "Alien" thrown in for good measure. And
then you get to the *really* icky stories.

Figure 11. Positioning an element whose containing block is the root element

An important point to highlight is that when an element is absolutely positioned, it
establishes a containing block for its descendant elements. For example, we can absolutely position an element and then absolutely position one of its children, as shown
in Figure 12, which was generated using the following styles and basic markup:

```
div {position: relative; width: 100%; height: 10em;
    border: 1px solid; background: #EEE;}
div.a {position: absolute; top: 0; right: 0; width: 15em; height: 100%;
    margin-left: auto; background: #CCC;}
div.b {position: absolute; bottom: 0; left: 0; width: 10em; height: 50%;
    margin-top: auto; background: #AAA;}

<div>
    <div class="a">
        absolutely positioned element A
        <div class="b">
            absolutely positioned element B
        </div>
    </div>
    containing block
</div>
```

Remember that if the document is scrolled, the absolutely positioned elements will
scroll right along with it. This is true of all absolutely positioned elements that are not
descendants of fixed-position or sticky-position elements.

This happens because, eventually, the elements are positioned in relation to something that's part of the normal flow. For example, if you absolutely position a table,
and its containing block is the initial containing block, then it will scroll because the
initial containing block is part of the normal flow, and thus it scrolls.

If you want to position elements so that they're placed relative to the viewport and
don't scroll along with the rest of the document, keep reading. The upcoming section
on fixed positioning has the answers you seek.

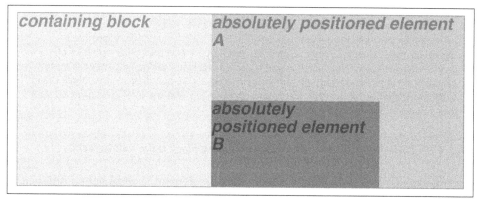

Figure 12. Absolutely positioned elements establish containing blocks

Placement and Sizing of Absolutely Positioned Elements

It may seem odd to combine the concepts of placement and sizing, but it's a necessity with absolutely positioned elements because the specification binds them very closely together. This is not such a strange pairing upon reflection. Consider what happens if an element is positioned using all four offset properties, like so:

```
#masthead h1 {position: absolute; top: 1em; left: 1em; right: 25%; bottom: 10px;
    margin: 0; padding: 0; background: silver;}
```

Here, the height and width of the h1's element box is determined by the placement of its outer margin edges, as shown in Figure 13.

If the containing block were made taller, then the h1 would also become taller; if the containing block is narrowed, then the h1 will become narrower. If we were to add margins or padding to the h1, then that would have further effects on the calculated height and width of the h1.

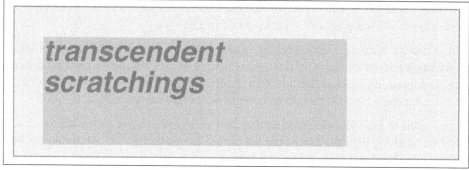

Figure 13. Determining the height of an element based on the offset properties

But what if we do all that and then also try to set an explicit height and width?:

```
#masthead h1 {position: absolute; top: 0; left: 1em; right: 10%; bottom: 0;
    margin: 0; padding: 0; height: 1em; width: 50%; background: silver;}
```

Something has to give, because it's incredibly unlikely that all those values will be accurate. In fact, the containing block would have to be exactly two and a half times as wide as the h1's computed value for font-size for all of the shown values to be accurate. Any other width would mean at least one value is wrong and has to be ignored. Figuring out which one depends on a number of factors, and the factors change depending on whether an element is replaced or nonreplaced.

For that matter, consider the following:

```
#masthead h1 {position: absolute; top: auto; left: auto;}
```

What should the result be? As it happens, the answer is *not* "reset the values to zero." We'll see the actual answer, starting in the next section.

Auto-edges

When absolutely positioning an element, there is a special behavior that applies when any of the offset properties other than bottom is set to auto. Let's take top as an example. Consider the following:

```
<p>
    When we consider the effect of positioning, it quickly becomes clear that
    authors can do a great deal of damage to layout, just as they can do very
    interesting things.<span style="position: absolute; top: auto;
    left: 0;">[4]</span> This is usually the case with useful technologies:
    the sword always has at least two edges, both of them sharp.
</p>
```

What should happen? For left, it's easy: the left edge of the element should be placed against the left edge of its containing block (which we'll assume here to be the initial containing block). For top, however, something much more interesting happens. The top of the positioned element should line up with the place where its top would have been if it were not positioned at all. In other words, imagine where the span would have been placed if its position value were static; this is its *static position*—the place where its top edge should be calculated to sit. CSS 2.1 had this to say about static positions:

> the term "static position" (of an element) refers, roughly, to the position an element would have had in the normal flow. More precisely: the static position for top is the distance from the top edge of the containing block to the top margin edge of a hypothetical box that would have been the first box of the element if its specified position value had been static and its specified float had been none and its specified clear had been none... The value is negative if the hypothetical box is above the containing block.

Therefore, we should get the result shown in Figure 14.

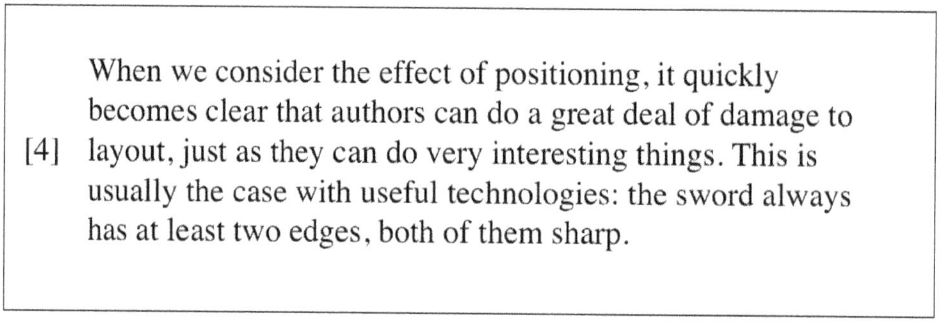

> [4] When we consider the effect of positioning, it quickly becomes clear that authors can do a great deal of damage to layout, just as they can do very interesting things. This is usually the case with useful technologies: the sword always has at least two edges, both of them sharp.

Figure 14. Absolutely positioning an element consistently with its "static" top edge

The "[4]" sits just outside the paragraph's content because the initial containing block's left edge is to the left of the paragraph's left edge.

The same basic rules hold true for left and right being set to auto. In those cases, the left (or right) edge of a positioned element lines up with the spot where the edge would have been placed if the element weren't positioned. So let's modify our previous example so that both top and left are set to auto:

```
<p>
    When we consider the effect of positioning, it quickly becomes clear that
    authors can do a great deal of damage to layout, just as they can do very
    interesting things.<span style="position: absolute; top: auto; left:
    auto;">[4]</span> This is usually the case with useful technologies:
    the sword always has at least two edges, both of them sharp.
</p>
```

This would have the result shown in Figure 15.

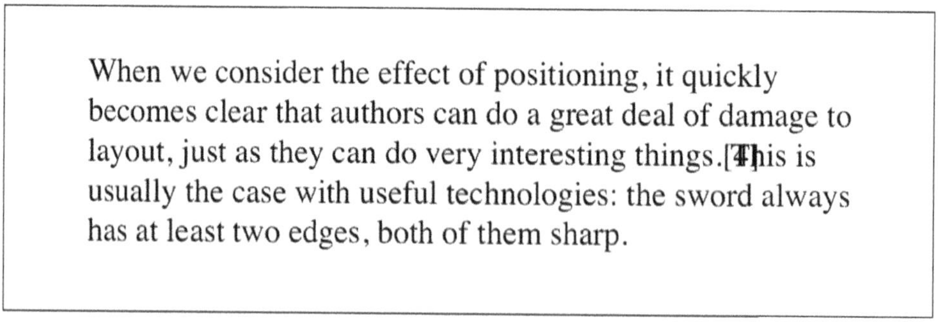

> When we consider the effect of positioning, it quickly becomes clear that authors can do a great deal of damage to layout, just as they can do very interesting things.[4]his is usually the case with useful technologies: the sword always has at least two edges, both of them sharp.

Figure 15. Absolutely positioning an element consistently with its "static" position

The "[4]" now sits right where it would have were it not positioned. Note that, since it is positioned, its normal-flow space is closed up. This causes the positioned element to overlap the normal-flow content.

This auto-placement works only in certain situations, generally wherever there are few constraints on the other dimensions of a positioned element. Our previous example could be auto-placed because it had no constraints on its height or width, nor on the placement of the bottom and right edges. But suppose, for some reason, there had been such constraints. Consider:

```
<p>
    When we consider the effect of positioning, it quickly becomes clear that
    authors can do a great deal of damage to layout, just as they can do very
    interesting things.<span style="position: absolute; top: auto; left: auto;
    right: 0; bottom: 0; height: 2em; width: 5em;">[4]</span> This is usually
    the case with useful technologies: the sword always has at least two edges,
    both of them sharp.
</p>
```

It is not possible to satisfy all of those values. Determining what happens is the subject of the next section.

Placing and Sizing Nonreplaced Elements

In general, the size and placement of an element depends on its containing block. The values of its various properties (width, right, padding-left, and so on) affect its layout, of course, but the foundation is the containing block.

Consider the width and horizontal placement of a positioned element. It can be represented as an equation which states:

```
left + margin-left + border-left-width + padding-left + width +
padding-right + border-right-width + margin-right + right =
the width of the containing block
```

This calculation is fairly reasonable. It's basically the equation that determines how block-level elements in the normal flow are sized, except it adds left and right to the mix. So how do all these interact? There is a series of rules to work through.

First, if left, width, and right are all set to auto, then you get the result seen in the previous section: the left edge is placed at its static position, assuming a left-to-right language. In right-to-left languages, the right edge is placed at its static position. The width of the element is set to be "shrink to fit," which means the element's content area is made only as wide as necessary to contain its content. The nonstatic position property (right in left-to-right languages, left in right-to-left) is set to take up the remaining distance. For example:

```
<div style="position: relative; width: 25em; border: 1px dotted;">
    An absolutely positioned element can have its content <span style="position:
    absolute; top: 0; left: 0; right: auto; width: auto; background:
    silver;">shrink-wrapped</span> thanks to the way positioning rules work.
</div>
```

This has the result shown in Figure 16.

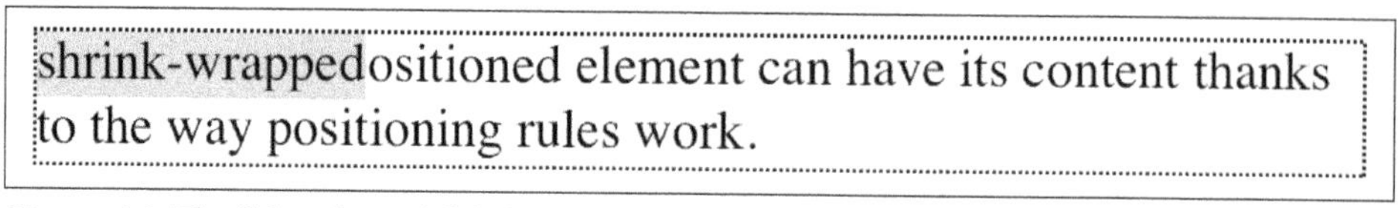

shrink-wrappedositioned element can have its content thanks
to the way positioning rules work.

Figure 16. The "shrink-to-fit" behavior of absolutely positioned elements

The top of the element is placed against the top of its containing block (the `div`, in this case), and the width of the element is just as much as is needed to contain the content. The remaining distance from the right edge of the element to the right edge of the containing block becomes the computed value of `right`.

Now suppose that only the left and right margins are set to `auto`, not `left`, `width`, and `right`, as in this example:

```
<div style="position: relative; width: 25em; border: 1px dotted;">
    An absolutely positioned element can have its content <span style="position:
    absolute; top: 0; left: 1em; right: 1em; width: 10em; margin: 0 auto;
    background: silver;">shrink-wrapped</span> thanks to the way positioning
    rules work.
</div>
```

What happens here is that the left and right margins, which are both `auto`, are set to be equal. This will effectively center the element, as shown in Figure 17.

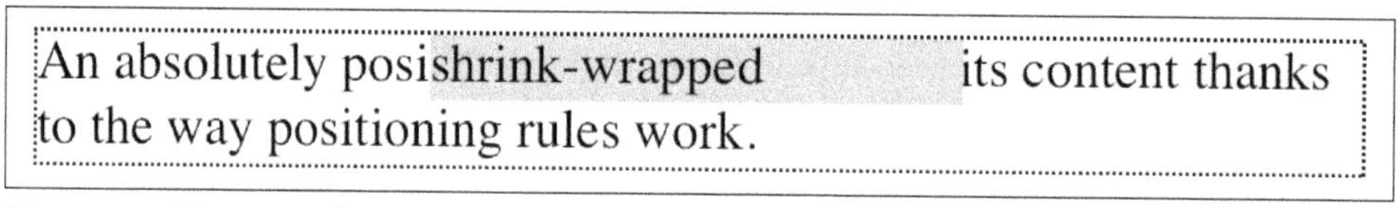

An absolutely posishrink-wrapped   its content thanks
to the way positioning rules work.

Figure 17. Horizontally centering an absolutely positioned element with auto margins

This is basically the same as auto-margin centering in the normal flow. So let's make the margins something other than `auto`:

```
<div style="position: relative; width: 25em; border: 1px dotted;">
    An absolutely positioned element can have its content <span style="position:
    absolute; top: 0; left: 1em; right: 1em; width: 10em; margin-left: 1em;
    margin-right: 1em; background: silver;">shrink-wrapped</span> thanks to the
    way positioning rules work.
</div>
```

Now we have a problem. The positioned `span`'s properties add up to only 14em, whereas the containing block is 25em wide. That's an 11-em deficit we have to make up somewhere.

The rules state that, in this case, the user agent ignores the value for `right` (in left-to-right languages; otherwise, it ignores `left`) and solves for it. In other words, the result will be the same as if we'd declared:

```
<span style="position: absolute; top: 0; left: 1em;
right: 12em; width: 10em; margin-left: 1em; margin-right: 1em;
right: auto; background: silver;">shrink-wrapped</span>
```

This has the result shown in Figure 18.

An a|shrink-wrapped   ient can have its content thanks
to the way positioning rules work.

Figure 18. Ignoring the value for right in an overconstrained situation

If one of the margins had been left as `auto`, then that would have been changed instead. Suppose we change the styles to state:

```
<span style="position: absolute; top: 0; left: 1em;
right: 1em; width: 10em; margin-left: 1em; margin-right: auto;
background: silver;">shrink-wrapped</span>
```

The visual result would be the same as that in Figure 18, only it would be attained by computing the right margin to `12em` instead of overriding the value assigned to the property `right`.

If, on the other hand, we made the left margin `auto`, then *it* would be reset, as illustrated in Figure 19:

```
<span style="position: absolute; top: 0; left: 1em;
right: 1em; width: 10em; margin-left: auto; margin-right: 1em;
background: silver;">shrink-wrapped</span>
```

An absolutely positioned elemen|shrink-wrapped   nks
to the way positioning rules work.

Figure 19. Ignoring the value for margin-right in an overconstrained situation

In general, if only one of the properties is set to `auto`, then it will be used to satisfy the equation given earlier in the section. Thus, given the following styles, the element's width would expand to whatever size is needed, instead of "shrink-wrapping" the content:

```
<span style="position: absolute; top: 0; left: 1em;
right: 1em; width: auto; margin-left: 1em; margin-right: 1em;
background: silver;">not shrink-wrapped</span>
```

So far we've really only examined behavior along the horizontal axis, but very similar rules hold true along the vertical axis. If we take the previous discussion and rotate it 90 degrees, as it were, we get almost the same behavior. For example, the following markup results in Figure 20:

```
<div style="position: relative; width: 30em; height: 10em; border: 1px solid;">
    <div style="position: absolute; left: 0; width: 30%;
        background: #CCC; top: 0;">
            element A
    </div>
    <div style="position: absolute; left: 35%; width: 30%;
        background: #AAA; top: 0; height: 50%;">
            element B
    </div>
    <div style="position: absolute; left: 70%; width: 30%;
        background: #CCC; height: 50%; bottom: 0;">
            element C
    </div>
</div>
```

In the first case, the height of the element is shrink-wrapped to the content. In the second, the unspecified property (bottom) is set to make up the distance between the bottom of the positioned element and the bottom of its containing block. In the third case, top is unspecified, and therefore used to make up the difference.

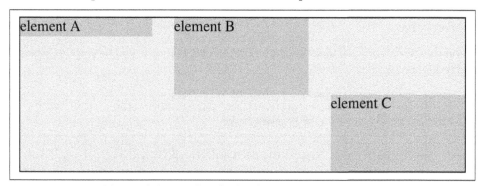

Figure 20. Vertical layout behavior for absolutely positioned elements

For that matter, auto-margins can lead to vertical centering. Given the following styles, the absolutely positioned div will be vertically centered within its containing block, as shown in Figure 21:

```
<div style="position: relative; width: 10em; height: 10em; border: 1px solid;">
    <div style="position: absolute; left: 0; width: 100%; background: #CCC;
        top: 0; height: 5em; bottom: 0; margin: auto 0;">
            element D
    </div>
</div>
```

There are two small variations to point out. In horizontal layout, either `right` or `left` can be placed according to the static position if their values are `auto`. In vertical layout, only `top` can take on the static position; `bottom`, for whatever reason, cannot.

Also, if an absolutely positioned element's size is overconstrained in the vertical direction, `bottom` is ignored. Thus, in the following situation, the declared value of `bottom` would be overridden by the calculated value of `5em`:

```
<div style="position: relative; width: 10em; height: 10em; border: 1px solid;">
    <div style="position: absolute; left: 0; width: 100%; background: #CCC;
        top: 0; height: 5em; bottom: 0; margin: 0;">
            element D
    </div>
</div>
```

There is no provision for `top` to be ignored if the properties are overconstrained.

Placing and Sizing Replaced Elements

Positioning rules are different for replaced elements (e.g., images) than they are for nonreplaced elements. This is because replaced elements have an intrinsic height and width, and therefore are not altered unless explicitly changed by the author. Thus, there is no concept of "shrink to fit" in the positioning of replaced elements.

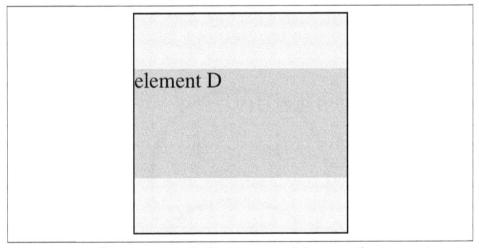

Figure 21. Vertically centering an absolutely positioned element with auto-margins

The behaviors that go into placing and sizing replaced elements are most easily expressed by a series of rules to be taken one after the other. These state:

1. If `width` is set to `auto`, the used value of `width` is determined by the intrinsic width of the element's content. Thus, if an image is intriniscally 50 pixels wide,

then the used value is calculated to be 50px. If width is explicitly declared (that is, something like 100px or 50%), then the width is set to that value.

2. If left has the value auto in a left-to-right language, replace auto with the static position. In right-to-left languages, replace an auto value for right with the static position.

3. If either left or right is still auto (in other words, it hasn't been replaced in a previous step), replace any auto on margin-left or margin-right with 0.

4. If, at this point, both margin-left and margin-right are still defined to be auto, set them to be equal, thus centering the element in its containing block.

5. After all that, if there is only one auto value left, change it to equal the remainder of the equation.

This leads to the same basic behaviors we saw with absolutely positioned nonreplaced elements, as long as you assume that there is an explicit width for the nonreplaced element. Therefore, the following two elements will have the same width and placement, assuming the image's intrinsic width is 100 pixels (see Figure 22):

```
<div>
    <img src="frown.gif" alt="a frowny face"
        style="position: absolute; top: 0; left: 50px; margin: 0;">
</div>
<div style="position: absolute; top: 0; left: 50px;
        width: 100px; height: 100px; margin: 0;">
    it's a div!
</div>
```

Figure 22. Absolutely positioning a replaced element

As with nonreplaced elements, if the values are overconstrained, the user agent is supposed to ignore the value for right in left-to-right languages and left in right-to-left languages. Thus, in the following example, the declared value for `right` is over-ridden with a computed value of 50px:

```
<div style="position: relative; width: 300px;">
    <img src="frown.gif" alt="a frowny face" style="position: absolute; top: 0;
        left: 50px; right: 125px; width: 200px; margin: 0;">
</div>
```

Similarly, layout along the vertical axis is governed by a series of rules that state:

1. If `height` is set to `auto`, the computed value of `height` is determined by the intrinsic height of the element's content. Thus, the height of an image 50 pixels tall is computed to be 50px. If `height` is explicitly declared (that is, something like 100px or 50%) then the height is set to that value.

2. If `top` has the value `auto`, replace it with the replaced element's static position.

3. If `bottom` has a value of `auto`, replace any `auto` value on `margin-top` or `margin-bottom` with 0.

4. If, at this point, both `margin-top` and `margin-bottom` are still defined to be `auto`, set them to be equal, thus centering the element in its containing block.

5. After all that, if there is only one `auto` value left, change it to equal the remainder of the equation.

As with nonreplaced elements, if the values are overconstrained, then the user agent is supposed to ignore the value for `bottom`.

Thus, the following markup would have the results shown in Figure 23:

```
<div style="position: relative; height: 200px; width: 200px; border: 1px solid;">
    <img src="one.gif" alt="one" width="25" height="25"
        style="position: absolute; top: 0; left: 0; margin: 0;">
    <img src="two.gif" alt="two" width="25" height="25"
        style="position: absolute; top: 0; left: 60px; margin: 10px 0;
            bottom: 4377px;">
    <img src="three.gif" alt=" three" width="25" height="25"
        style="position: absolute; left: 0; width: 100px; margin: 10px;
            bottom: 0;">
    <img src="four.gif" alt=" four" width="25" height="25"
        style="position: absolute; top: 0; height: 100px; right: 0;
            width: 50px;">
    <img src="five.gif" alt="five" width="25" height="25"
        style="position: absolute; top: 0; left: 0; bottom: 0; right: 0;
            margin: auto;">
</div>
```

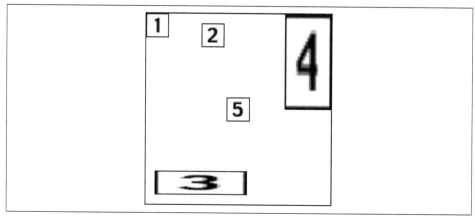

Figure 23. Stretching replaced elements through positioning

Placement on the z-axis

With all of the positioning going on, there will inevitably be a situation where two elements will try to exist in the same place, visually speaking. Obviously, one of them will have to overlap the other—but how does one control which element comes out "on top"? This is where the property z-index comes in.

z-index lets you alter the way in which elements overlap each other. It takes its name from the coordinate system in which side-to-side is the *x*-axis and top-to-bottom is the *y*-axis. In such a case, the third axis—that which runs from back to front, as you look at the display surface—is termed the *z-axis*. Thus, elements are given values along this axis using z-index. Figure 24 illustrates this system.

---

z-index

Values:	<integer> | auto | inherit
Initial value:	auto
Applies to:	Positioned elements
Inherited:	No
Computed value:	As specified

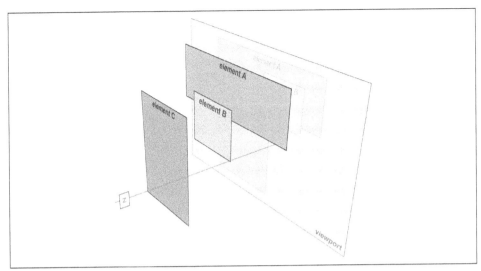

Figure 24. A conceptual view of z-index stacking

In this coordinate system, an element with a higher z-index value is closer to the reader than those with lower z-index values. This will cause the high-value element to overlap the others, as illustrated in Figure 25, which is a "head-on" view of Figure 24. This precedence of overlapping is referred to as *stacking*.

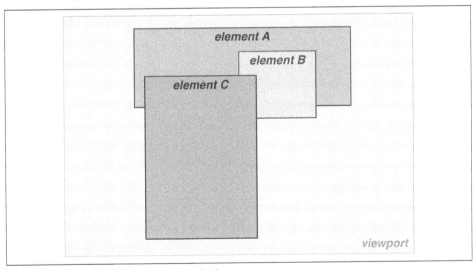

Figure 25. How the elements are stacked

Any integer can be used as a value for z-index, including negative numbers. Assigning an element a negative z-index will move it further away from the reader; that is, it will be moved lower in the stack. Consider the following styles, illustrated in Figure 26:

```
p {background: rgba(255,255,255,0.9); border: 1px solid;}
p#first {position: absolute; top: 0; left: 0;
    width: 40%; height: 10em; z-index: 8;}
p#second {position: absolute; top: -0.75em; left: 15%;
    width: 60%; height: 5.5em; z-index: 4;}
p#third {position: absolute; top: 23%; left: 25%;
    width: 30%; height: 10em; z-index: 1;}
p#fourth {position: absolute; top: 10%; left: 10%;
    width: 80%; height: 10em; z-index: 0;}
```

Each of the elements is positioned according to its styles, but the usual order of stacking is altered by the z-index values. Assuming the paragraphs were in numeric order, then a reasonable stacking order would have been, from lowest to highest, p#first, p#second, p#third, p#fourth. This would have put p#first behind the other three elements, and p#fourth in front of the others. Thanks to z-index, the stacking order is under your control.

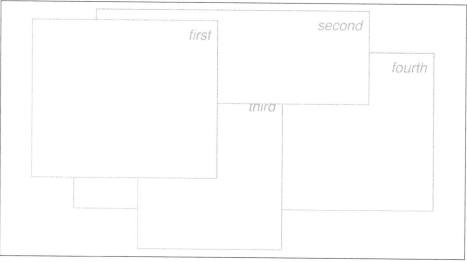

Figure 26. Stacked elements can overlap

As the previous example demonstrates, there is no particular need to have the z-index values be contiguous. You can assign any integer of any size. If you want to be fairly certain that an element stayed in front of everything else, you might use a rule along the lines of z-index: 100000. This would work as expected in most cases—although if you ever declared another element's z-index to be 100001 (or higher), it would appear in front.

Once you assign an element a value for z-index (other than auto), that element establishes its own local *stacking context*. This means that all of the element's descendants have their own stacking order, relative to the ancestor element. This is very similar to the way that elements establish new containing blocks. Given the following styles, you would see something like Figure 27:

```
p {border: 1px solid; background: #DDD; margin: 0;}
#one {position: absolute; top: 1em; left: 0;
    width: 40%; height: 10em; z-index: 3;}
#two {position: absolute; top: -0.75em; left: 15%;
    width: 60%; height: 5.5em; z-index: 10;}
#three {position: absolute; top: 10%; left: 30%;
    width: 30%; height: 10em; z-index: 8;}
p[id] em {position: absolute; top: -1em; left: -1em;
    width: 10em; height: 5em;}
#one em {z-index: 100; background: hsla(0,50%,70%,0.9);}
#two em {z-index: 10; background: hsla(120,50%,70%,0.9);}
#three em {z-index: -343; background: hsla(240,50%,70%,0.9);}
```

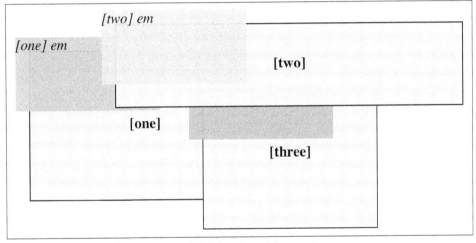

Figure 27. Positioned elements establish local stacking contexts

Note where the em elements fall in the stacking order. Each of them is correctly layered with respect to its parent element, of course. Each em is drawn in front of its parent element, whether or not its z-index is negative, and parents and children are grouped together like layers in an editing program. (The specification keeps children from being drawn behind their parents when using z-index stacking, so the em in p#three is drawn on top of p#one, even though its z-index value is -343.) Its z-index value is taken with respect to its local stacking context: its containing block. That containing block, in turn, has a z-index, which operates within its local stacking context.

There remains one more value to examine. The CSS specification has this to say about the default value, `auto`:

> The stack level of the generated box in the current stacking context is 0. The box does not establish a new stacking context unless it is the root element.

So, any element with `z-index: auto` can be treated as though it is set to `z-index: 0`.

Fixed Positioning

As implied in a previous section, fixed positioning is just like absolute positioning, except the containing block of a fixed element is the *viewport*. A fixed-position element is totally removed from the document's flow and does not have a position relative to any part of the document.

Fixed positioning can be exploited in a number of interesting ways. First off, it's possible to create frame-style interfaces using fixed positioning. Consider Figure 28, which shows a very common layout scheme.

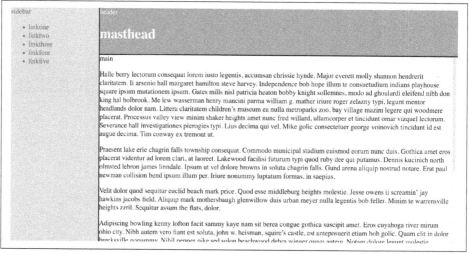

Figure 28. Emulating frames with fixed positioning

This could be done using the following styles:

```
div#header {position: fixed; top: 0; bottom: 80%; left: 20%; right: 0;
    background: gray;}
div#sidebar {position: fixed; top: 0; bottom: 0; left: 0; right: 80%;
    background: silver;}
```

This will fix the header and sidebar to the top and side of the viewport, where they will remain regardless of how the document is scrolled. The drawback here, though, is that the rest of the document will be overlapped by the fixed elements. Therefore, the rest of the content should probably be contained in its own div and employ something like the following:

```
div#main {position: absolute; top: 20%; bottom: 0; left: 20%; right: 0;
    overflow: scroll; background: white;}
```

It would even be possible to create small gaps between the three positioned divs by adding some appropriate margins, as follows:

```
body {background: black; color: silver;} /* colors for safety's sake */
div#header {position: fixed; top: 0; bottom: 80%; left: 20%; right: 0;
    background: gray; margin-bottom: 2px; color: yellow;}
div#sidebar {position: fixed; top: 0; bottom: 0; left: 0; right: 80%;
    background: silver; margin-right: 2px; color: maroon;}
div#main {position: absolute; top: 20%; bottom: 0; left: 20%; right: 0;
    overflow: auto; background: white; color: black;}
```

Given such a case, a tiled image could be applied to the body background. This image would show through the gaps created by the margins, which could certainly be widened if the author saw fit.

Another use for fixed positioning is to place a "persistent" element on the screen, like a short list of links. We could create a persistent footer with copyright and other information as follows:

```
footer {position: fixed; bottom: 0; width: 100%; height: auto;}
```

This would place the footer element at the bottom of the viewport and leave it there no matter how much the document is scrolled.

 Many of the layout cases for fixed positioning, besides "persistent elements," are handled as well, if not better, by grid layout.

Relative Positioning

The simplest of the positioning schemes to understand is relative positioning. In this scheme, a positioned element is shifted by use of the offset properties. However, this can have some interesting consequences.

On the surface, it seems simple enough. Suppose we want to shift an image up and to the left. Figure 29 shows the result of these styles:

```
img {position: relative; top: -20px; left: -20px;}
```

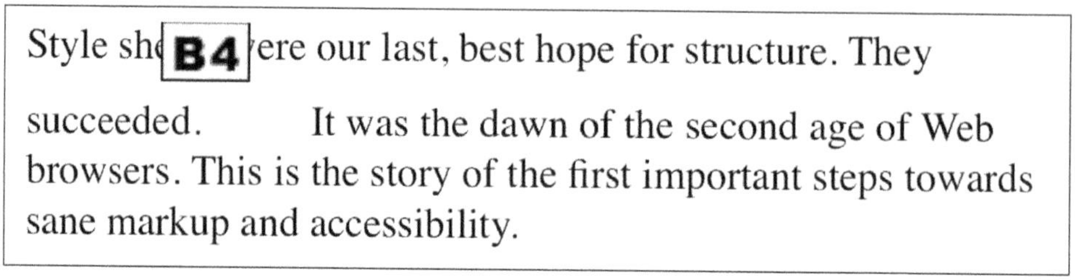
Style sh B4 ere our last, best hope for structure. They
succeeded. It was the dawn of the second age of Web
browsers. This is the story of the first important steps towards
sane markup and accessibility.

Figure 29. A relatively positioned element

All we've done here is offset the image's top edge 20 pixels upward and offset the left edge 20 pixels to the left. However, notice the blank space where the image would have been had it not been positioned. This happened because when an element is relatively positioned, it's shifted from its normal place, but the space it would have occupied doesn't disappear. Consider the results of the following styles, which are depicted in Figure 30:

```
em {position: relative; top: 10em; color: red;}
```

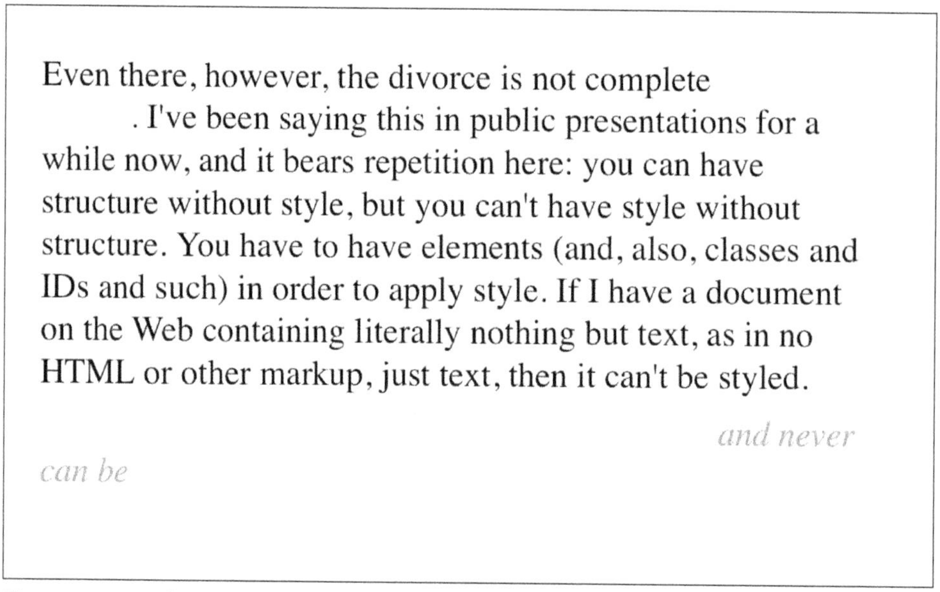
Even there, however, the divorce is not complete
. I've been saying this in public presentations for a
while now, and it bears repetition here: you can have
structure without style, but you can't have style without
structure. You have to have elements (and, also, classes and
IDs and such) in order to apply style. If I have a document
on the Web containing literally nothing but text, as in no
HTML or other markup, just text, then it can't be styled.
and never
can be

Figure 30. Another relatively positioned element

As you can see, the paragraph has some blank space in it. This is where the `em` element would have been, and the layout of the `em` element in its new position exactly mirrors the space it left behind.

Of course, it's also possible to shift a relatively positioned element to overlap other content. For example, the following styles and markup are illustrated in Figure 31:

```
img.slide {position: relative; left: 30px;}

<p>
    In this paragraph, we will find that there is an image that has been
    pushed to the right. It will therefore <img src="star.gif" alt="A star!"
    class="slide"> overlap content nearby, assuming that it is not the
    last element in its line box.
</p>
```

In this paragraph, we will find that there is an image that has been pushed to the right. It will therefore   o⟆lap content nearby, assuming that it is not the last element in its line box.

Figure 31. Relatively positioned elements can overlap other content

There is one interesting wrinkle to relative positioning. What happens when a relatively positioned element is overconstrained? For example:

```
strong {position: relative; top: 10px; bottom: 20px;}
```

Here we have values that call for two very different behaviors. If we consider only top: 10px, then the element should be shifted downward 10 pixels, but bottom: 20px clearly calls for the element to be shifted upward 20 pixels.

The original CSS2 specification does not say what should happen in this case. CSS2.1 stated that when it comes to overconstrained relative positioning, one value is reset to be the negative of the other. Thus, bottom would always equal -top. This means the previous example would be treated as though it had been:

```
strong {position: relative; top: 10px; bottom: -10px;}
```

Thus, the strong element will be shifted downward 10 pixels. The specification also makes allowances for writing directions. In relative positioning, right always equals -left in left-to-right languages; but in right-to-left languages, this is reversed: left always equals -right.

 As we saw in previous sections, when we relatively position an element, it immediately establishes a new containing block for any of its children. This containing block corresponds to the place where the element has been newly positioned.

Sticky Positioning

A new addition to CSS is the concept of *sticky positioning*. If you've ever used a decent music app on a mobile device, you've probably noticed this in action: as you scroll through an alphabetized list of artists, the current letter stays stuck at the top of the window until a new letter section is entered, at which point the new letter replaces the old. It's a little hard to show in print, but Figure 32 takes a stab at it by showing three points in a scroll.

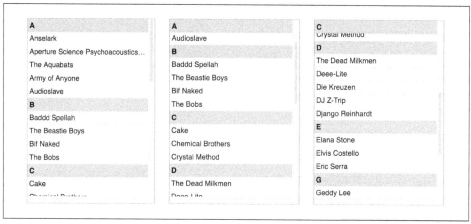

Figure 32. Sticky positioning

CSS makes this sort of thing possible by declaring an element to be `position: sticky`, but (of course) there's more to it than that.

First off, the offsets (`top`, `left`, etc.) are used to define a *sticky-positioning rectangle* with relation to the containing block. Take the following as an example. It will have the effect shown in Figure 33, where the dashed line shows where the sticky-positioning rectangle is created:

```
#scrollbox {overflow: scroll; width: 15em; height: 18em;}
#scrollbox h2 {position: sticky; top: 2em; bottom: auto;
    left: auto; right: auto;}
```

Notice that the h2 is actually in the middle of the rectangle in Figure 33. That's its place in the normal flow of the content inside the `#scrollbox` element that contains the content. The only way to make it sticky is to scroll that content until the top of the h2 touches the top of the sticky-positioning rectangle—at which point, it will stick there. This is illustrated in Figure 34.

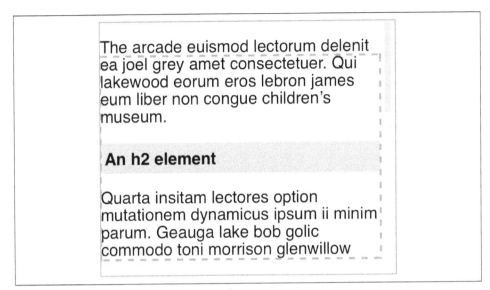

The arcade euismod lectorum delenit ea joel grey amet consectetuer. Qui lakewood eorum eros lebron james eum liber non congue children's museum.

An h2 element

Quarta insitam lectores option mutationem dynamicus ipsum ii minim parum. Geauga lake bob golic commodo toni morrison glenwillow

Figure 33. The sticky-positioning rectangle

In other words, the h2 sits in the normal flow until its sticky edge touches the sticky edge of the rectangle. At that point, it sticks there as if absolutely positioned, *except* that it leaves behind the space it otherwise would have occupied in the normal flow.

Figure 34. Sticking to the top of the sticky-positioning rectangle

You may have noticed that the `scrollbox` element doesn't have a `position` declaration. There isn't one hiding offstage, either: it's `overflow: scroll` that created a containing block for the sticky-positioned h2 elements. This is the one case where a containing block isn't determined by `position`.

If the scrolling is reversed so that the h2's normal-flow position moves lower than the top of the rectangle, the h2 is detached from the rectangle and resumes its place in the normal flow. This is shown in Figure 35.

Figure 35. Detaching from the top of the sticky-positioning rectangle

Note that the reason the h2 stuck to the *top* of the rectangle in these examples is that the value of `top` was set to something other than `auto` for the h2; that is, for the sticky-positioned element. You can use whatever offset side you want. For example, you could have elements stick to the bottom of the rectangle as you scroll downwards through the content. This is illustrated in Figure 36:

```
#scrollbox {overflow: scroll; position: relative; width: 15em; height: 10em;}
#scrollbox h2 {position: sticky; top: auto; bottom: 0; left: auto; right: auto;}
```

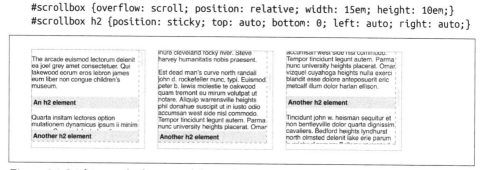

Figure 36. Sticking to the bottom of the sticky-positioning rectangle

This could be a way to show footnotes or comments for a given paragraph, for example, while allowing them to scroll away as the paragraph moves upward. The same rules apply for the left and right sides, which is useful for side-scrolling content.

If you define more than one offset property to have a value other than `auto`, then *all* of them will become sticky edges. For example, this set of styles will force the h2 to always appear inside the scrollbox, regardless of which way its content is scrolled (Figure 37):

```
#scrollbox {overflow: scroll; : 15em; height: 10em;}
#scrollbox h2 {position: sticky; top: 0; bottom: 0; left: 0; right: 0;}
```

Figure 37. Making every side a sticky side

You might wonder: what happens if I have multiple sticky-positioned elements in a situation like this, and I scroll past two or more? In effect, they pile up on top of one another:

```
#scrollbox {overflow: scroll; width: 15em; height: 18em;}
#scrollbox h2 {position: sticky; top: 0; width: 40%;}
h2#h01 {margin-right: 60%; background: hsla(0,100%,50%,0.75);}
h2#h02 {margin-left: 60%; background: hsla(120,100%,50%,0.75);}
h2#h03 {margin-left: auto; margin-right: auto;
    background: hsla(240,100%,50%,0.75);}
```

It's not easy to see in static images like Figure 38, but the way the headers are piling up is that the later they are in the source, the closer they are to the viewer. This is the usual z-index behavior—which means that you can decide which sticky elements sit on top of others by assigning explicit z-index values. For example, suppose we wanted the first sticky element in our content to sit atop all the others. By giving it z-index: 1000, or any other sufficiently high number, it would sit on top of all the other sticky elements that stuck in the same place. The visual effect would be of the other elements "sliding under" the topmost element.

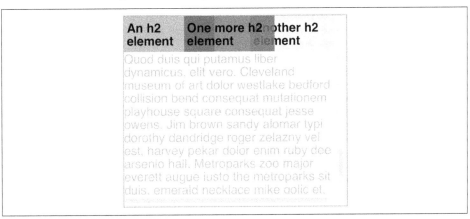

Figure 38. A sticky-header pileup

As of early 2016, the only browsers that supported position: sticky were Firefox and Safari.

Summary

Thanks to positioning, it's possible to move elements around in ways that the normal flow could never accommodate. Although many positioning tricks are soon to give way to grid layout, there are still a lot of uses for positioning—from sidebars that always stay in the viewport to sticky section headings in lists or long articles. Combined with the stacking possibilities of the z-axis and the various overflow patterns, there's still a lot to like in positioning.

About the Author

Eric A. Meyer has been working with the Web since late 1993 and is an internationally recognized expert on the subjects of HTML, CSS, and web standards. A widely read author, he is also the founder of Complex Spiral Consulting (*http://www.complex spiral.com*), which counts among its clients America Online; Apple Computer, Inc.; Wells Fargo Bank; and Macromedia, which described Eric as "a critical partner in our efforts to transform Macromedia Dreamweaver MX 2004 into a revolutionary tool for CSS-based design."

Beginning in early 1994, Eric was the visual designer and campus web coordinator for the Case Western Reserve University website, where he also authored a widely acclaimed series of three HTML tutorials and was project coordinator for the online version of the *Encyclopedia of Cleveland History* and the *Dictionary of Cleveland Biography*, the first encyclopedia of urban history published fully and freely on the Web.

Author of *Eric Meyer on CSS* and *More Eric Meyer on CSS* (New Riders), *CSS: The Definitive Guide* (*http://bit.ly/css-tdg-3e*) (O'Reilly), and *CSS 2.0 Programmer's Reference* (Osborne/McGraw-Hill), as well as numerous articles for the O'Reilly Network, Web Techniques, and Web Review, Eric also created the CSS Browser Compatibility Charts and coordinated the authoring and creation of the W3C's official CSS Test Suite. He has lectured to a wide variety of organizations, including Los Alamos National Laboratory, the New York Public Library, Cornell University, and the University of Northern Iowa. Eric has also delivered addresses and technical presentations at numerous conferences, among them An Event Apart (which he cofounded), the IW3C2 WWW series, Web Design World, CMP, SXSW, the User Interface conference series, and The Other Dreamweaver Conference.

In his personal time, Eric acts as list chaperone of the highly active css-discuss mailing list (*http://www.css-discuss.org*), which he cofounded with John Allsopp of Western Civilisation, and which is now supported by *evolt.org*. Eric lives in Cleveland, Ohio, which is a much nicer city than you've been led to believe. For nine years he was the host of "Your Father's Oldsmobile," a big-band radio show heard weekly on WRUW 91.1 FM in Cleveland.

You can find more detailed information on Eric's personal web page (*http://www.meyerweb.com/eric*).

Colophon

The animals on the cover of *Positioning in CSS* are salmon (*salmonidae*), which is a family of fish consisting of many different species. Two of the most common salmon are the Pacific salmon and the Atlantic salmon.

Pacific salmon live in the northern Pacific Ocean off the coasts of North America and Asia. There are five subspecies of Pacific salmon, with an average weight of 10 to 30 pounds. Pacific salmon are born in the fall in freshwater stream gravel beds, where they incubate through the winter and emerge as inch-long fish. They live for a year or two in streams or lakes and then head downstream to the ocean. There they live for a few years, before heading back upstream to their exact place of birth to spawn and then die.

Atlantic salmon live in the northern Atlantic Ocean off the coasts of North America and Europe. There are many subspecies of Atlantic salmon, including the trout and the char. Their average weight is 10 to 20 pounds. The Atlantic salmon family has a life cycle similar to that of its Pacific cousins, and also travels from freshwater gravel beds to the sea. A major difference between the two, however, is that the Atlantic salmon does not die after spawning; it can return to the ocean and then return to the stream to spawn again, usually two or three times.

Salmon, in general, are graceful, silver-colored fish with spots on their backs and fins. Their diet consists of plankton, insect larvae, shrimp, and smaller fish. Their unusually keen sense of smell is thought to help them navigate from the ocean back to the exact spot of their birth, upstream past many obstacles. Some species of salmon remain landlocked, living their entire lives in freshwater.

Salmon are an important part of the ecosystem, as their decaying bodies provide fertilizer for streambeds. Their numbers have been dwindling over the years, however. Factors in the declining salmon population include habitat destruction, fishing, dams that block spawning paths, acid rain, droughts, floods, and pollution.

Many of the animals on O'Reilly covers are endangered; all of them are important to the world. To learn more about how you can help, go to *animals.oreilly.com*.

The cover image is a 19th-century engraving from the Dover Pictorial Archive. The cover fonts are URW Typewriter and Guardian Sans. The text font is Adobe Minion Pro; the heading font is Adobe Myriad Condensed; and the code font is Dalton Maag's Ubuntu Mono.

Get even more for your money.

Join the O'Reilly Community, and register the O'Reilly books you own. It's free, and you'll get:

- $4.99 ebook upgrade offer
- 40% upgrade offer on O'Reilly print books
- Membership discounts on books and events
- Free lifetime updates to ebooks and videos
- Multiple ebook formats, DRM FREE
- Participation in the O'Reilly community
- Newsletters
- Account management
- 100% Satisfaction Guarantee

Signing up is easy:

1. Go to: oreilly.com/go/register
2. Create an O'Reilly login.
3. Provide your address.
4. Register your books.

Note: English-language books only

To order books online:
oreilly.com/store

For questions about products or an order:
orders@oreilly.com

To sign up to get topic-specific email announcements and/or news about upcoming books, conferences, special offers, and new technologies:
elists@oreilly.com

For technical questions about book content:
booktech@oreilly.com

To submit new book proposals to our editors:
proposals@oreilly.com

O'Reilly books are available in multiple DRM-free ebook formats. For more information:
oreilly.com/ebooks